SEVEN MASSES

Recent Researches in the Music of the Renaissance is one of four quarterly series (Middle Ages and Early Renaissance; Renaissance; Baroque Era; Classical Era) which make public the early music that is being brought to light in the course of current musicological research.

Each volume is devoted to works by a single composer or in a single genre of composition, chosen because of their potential interest to scholars and performers, and prepared for publication according to the standards that govern the making of all reliable historical editions.

Subscribers to this series, as well as patrons of subscribing institutions, are invited to apply for information about the "Copyright-Sharing Policy" of A-R Editions, Inc. under which the contents of this volume may be reproduced free of charge for performance use.

Correspondence should be addressed:

A-R Editions, Inc.
315 West Gorham Street
Madison, Wisconsin 53703

RECENT RESEARCHES IN THE MUSIC OF THE RENAISSANCE • VOLUME XXXII

Vincenzo Ruffo

SEVEN MASSES

Part I: Three Early Masses

Edited by Lewis Lockwood

A-R EDITIONS, INC. • MADISON

Copyright © 1979, A-R Editions, Inc.

SEVEN MASSES is, to the best knowledge of the publisher,
the first edition of music to have been completely engraved by
computerized photocomposition. Encoding was begun in October 1977,
and engraving was completed in May 1979.

ISSN 0486-123X

ISBN 0-89579-118-8 (Set, Parts I and II)
ISBN 0-89579-119-6 (Part I)

Library of Congress Cataloging in Publication Data:

Ruffo, Vincenzo, 16th cent.
    Seven Masses.

    (Recent researches in the music of the Renaissance ;
v. 32-33 ISSN 0486-123X)
    For 4-5 voices; Latin words.
    CONTENTS: Pt. 1. Three early Masses.—Pt. 2.
Four later Masses.
    1. Masses—Vocal scores. I. Lockwood, Lewis.
II. Series.
M2.R2384   vol. 32-33   [M2011]   780'.903'1s   [783.2'1'54]
ISBN 0-89579-118-8   79-17464

Contents

Preface

Introduction

This edition of seven Masses by the sixteenth-century North Italian composer Vincenzo Ruffo (ca. 1508-1587) aims to convey a representative selection of his works in this genre, to show an evolution of style, and to illustrate a thesis. The thesis is this: more than any other Italian composer of sacred music during the period from 1540 to 1580 (not excepting Palestrina, Animuccia, and Porta), Ruffo in his Masses undergoes a passage from one concept of composition to a quite different one. This process reflects not simply his personal development as a composer, but also the influence of close contact with men and events of the Counter-Reformation, above all the Milanese Archbishop and Cardinal Carlo Borromeo (1538-1584). For almost a decade (from 1563 to 1572) Ruffo served as Master of the Chapel of the Cathedral of Milan when Borromeo was its Archbishop. In prefaces to his later publications of sacred music, Ruffo repeatedly refers to Borromeo as his "dearest Lord and Master" and invokes the decrees of the Council of Trent as the basis for his new style in Mass composition. The three Masses of Part I of this edition are representative early works, all written prior to Ruffo's contacts with Borromeo and the Tridentine principles; stemming from a period of prolific composition in both sacred and secular music, these Masses display Ruffo's early command of contemporary techniques involving imitative counterpoint and derivation from models. The four later works, contained in Part II of this edition, are all from publications of 1570 or later, and they show the sharply defined change of style. The first two Masses of the later group (*Quarti toni* and *Octavi toni*) are from Ruffo's experimental volume of four-voice Masses published in 1570; the two works that follow (*Missa de De profundis* and *Missa Sanctissimae Trinitatis*) show efforts to loosen and modify the severe homophony of the 1570 group while maintaining as much as possible of the "intelligible" style (see below), especially in the long movements. Since I have discussed these works and their biographical and historical context at length elsewhere, commentary here will be limited to brief descriptive annotation and to the Critical Notes suited to this edition.[1]

Ruffo's Career: A New Conspectus

Vincenzo Ruffo is doubtless the best-known Veronese composer of the sixteenth century and one of the most versatile and productive masters of sacred and secular polyphonic genres. Until recently all we knew of his youth was that from 1521 to 1534 Ruffo was trained in the *Scuola degli Accoliti* of the Cathedral of Verona, and apparently from 1531 until 1534 he was one of twelve *cappellani accoliti* (cathedral singers). This *scuola* was an important institution for the training of musicians. Among several *scuole* in northern Italy that had come into existence in the mid-fifteenth century, it was distinctive in its continuity as a didactic center where native Italian musicians could receive instruction. The *Scuola's* music master for many years was the organist and theorist Biagio Rossetti, whose high standards for performance are mirrored in his *Libellus de rudimentis musices* (1529) and whose effective role as teacher and mentor was undoubtedly supported by Bishop Gian Matteo Giberti, an influential precursor of reforms later associated with the Council of Trent.

Important recent discoveries by Enrico Paganuzzi in local archives include a document of 27 October 1520 which confirms Giuseppe Turrini's earlier finding that in 1521 Ruffo became a member of the *Scuola*;[2] but the document also shows that he was indeed of Veronese origin and was the son of a local notary.[3] That Ruffo's mature connections with Verona remained strong had been evident from what we already knew of his periodic returns to Verona from other posts at later points in his long career. Thanks to Paganuzzi it is now clear that, despite his early role as acolyte and *cappellano*, Ruffo did not in fact take vows as a priest (this disconfirms my earlier supposition that he did do so), but by 1555 was a married man with two sons aged nineteen and sixteen. A "correction" made by an apparently contemporary hand in the 1555 document, altering Ruffo's age from "47" to "40," scarcely seems plausible, since if he had been forty in 1555, he would have been only five years old in 1520 when he was chosen as an acolyte; but if the figure "47" is trustworthy, it provides the first contemporary evidence for the year of birth, placing it in 1508 (I had formerly assumed "about 1510," based on other evidence). Ruffo's training with Rossetti probably resulted in much composition as early as the 1530s. In 1541 Ruffo left Verona to join the service of the flamboyant nobleman Alfonso d'Avalos, Marchese del Vasto, who was then Governor-General of Milan under the Emperor Charles V. Ruffo apparently remained with d'Avalos until about 1546.[4]

In Milan in 1542, under Alfonso's patronage, Ruffo was able to publish his first works (the *Alma redemptoris mater* Mass included here, and the *Primo Libro de Motetti a Cinque Voci*). Ruffo's motet volume, published at Milan in 1542, is among the earliest of such collections (sets of motets by a single composer, as opposed to anthologies containing motets by a variety of composers) to be published. In 1539, Scotto in Venice had issued the earliest individual motet collections, those of Jacquet of Mantua, Adrian Willaert, and Nicolas Gombert—thus honoring the principal musicians associated with Mantua, Venice, and, in Gombert, the Milan of Charles V, as is clear from the dedication of the Gombert print, *Motecta . . . Liber Primus*, to this same Milanese patron Alfonso d'Avalos. That motets by Ruffo formed part of the repertory of the musical circles around d'Avalos is already clear. Joseph Schmidt-Görg, modern editor of the works of Gombert, has recently acknowledged Ruffo's authorship of six motets left anonymous in Gombert's five-voice collection of 1541. Although this volume presents Gombert as the leading figure, only a small number of its motets are definitely by him; others are ascribed to Jacquet and Morales, while of the remaining eleven anonymous motets, the six mentioned above were then published the next year in Ruffo's own motet book of 1542, which is entirely devoted to works ascribed to him.[5]

Ruffo was probably in d'Avalos's service until 1546; thereafter, the stages of his career are clearly evident. From 1547 to 1563 he was again in Verona, first in close connection with the local secular music academy, the *Accademia Filarmonica* (he became its music master in 1551), and then as music master at the Cathedral. During this period Ruffo was especially productive as a madrigalist, publishing nine collections between 1545 and 1556.[6] From these years also come a second volume of motets (1555), a book of Magnificats (1559), and Ruffo's own first book of Masses (1557) from which two works are included here (*Missa Quem dicunt homines* and *Missa Aspice domine*). At this time he was also the teacher of the prolific composer Giammateo Asola and of Marc'Antonio Ingegneri, who, in turn, became the teacher of Claudio Monteverdi.

Between 1563 and 1572 Ruffo was music master at the great Cathedral of Milan, where from 1565 on he was under the immediate personal influence of Carlo Borromeo, Archbishop of Milan and one of the most powerful leaders of the movement toward reform of the Catholic Church in the wake of the Council of Trent (1545-1563). Before Borromeo left Rome in 1565 to serve in Milan, he and Cardinal Vitellozzo Vitelli had held a trial of sacred music by several composers to see whether the texts could be set in such a way as to make the words intelligible; it was for this trial, according to the conjecture of Palestrina's biographer Giuseppe Baini, that the *Missa Papae Marcelli* was written.[7] Although there is no clear proof regarding his participation, Palestrina may have taken part, and it is likely that the Mass named for Pope Marcellus is a product of the same conditions that prompted Ruffo to compose his "reform" Masses. Letters concerning Ruffo's music were written by Borromeo to his vicar in Milan just before the trial of 1565, in which he directly commissioned that a Mass be written "which should be as clear as possible, and send it to me here." Shortly afterward Borromeo reminded his vicar that he was waiting for Ruffo's Mass, which had clearly been promised, and suggested that a similar work be written "by don Nicola [Nicola Vicentino] who favors chromatic music." There is no evidence that Vicentino ever followed this suggestion. In Ruffo's case, however, we know that his published Masses of 1570 (two of which, the *Missa Quarti toni* and the *Missa Octavi toni*, are included here) were written expressly to fulfill Borromeo's commission. In his preface to the 1570 volume Ruffo makes clear that he took on this special task:

> which Cardinal Borromeo had formerly imposed on me, that in accordance with the decrees of the Most Holy Council of Trent I was to compose some Masses that should avoid everything of a profane and idle manner in worship. . . . Accordingly . . . I composed one Mass in this way: so that the numbers of the syllables and the voices and tones together should be clearly and distinctly understood by the pious listeners . . . later, imitating that example, I more readily and easily composed other Masses of the same type. . . .[8]

In several later publications Ruffo again declares his allegiance to the principles of textual clarity and avoidance of secular elements, taking pride in his relationship to Borromeo and repeating his intention to show that "in the divine offices one could introduce a kind of music that would be serious, sweet, and devout, and that would entirely conform to the purposes of the holy Council of Trent . . ." (preface to his *Salmi Suavissimi et Devotissimi a Cinque Voci*, 1574). A similarly explicit statement is made in the Discourse to the Reader written by Ruffo to preface his *Quarto Libro di Messe a Sei Voci,* also of 1574, which includes the *Missa Sanctissimae Trinitatis.* The *Missa Sanctissimae Trinitatis* is printed in the present edition on pp. 72 ff., Part II.

After this centrally important period in Milan under Borromeo, Ruffo spent five years (from 1573 to 1577) at the Cathedral of Pistoia. From 1578 to 1580 he was, apparently, again in Verona; and his last post (from 1580 to 1587) was at the small church of San Nicolò in the town of Sacile in Friuli, where he died, as his memorial stone says, "in extremum usque senium." If the newly assumed birthdate (see above) is correct, he was seventy-nine years old when he died, a ripe age for the time.

Ruffo had pursued his career in a wide area of northern Italy, including Tuscan Pistoia, and he had maintained a steady and prolific output with many publications in several important genres. He had also been conspicuous for his readiness and ability to supply effective polyphonic works for a variety of secular and sacred purposes and for patrons of varied interests. In later years, this tendency was to be channeled with single-minded concentration into the composition of sacred music, much of which was written in response to avowed aims of the Counter-Reformation. The seven works presented in this edition exemplify the various stages of this development in Ruffo's Mass composition.

The Masses

Three Early Masses

Each Mass is transcribed from its earliest printed source unless otherwise indicated.

Missa Alma redemptoris mater

Published in 1542 in an anthology of Masses for equal voices (RISM 1542[3]), this work is the first polyphonic Mass setting by a native Italian composer ever printed, antedating by six years the collection of Masses by Gaspar de Albertis, choirmaster at Bergamo.[9] The 1542 collection places "Ruffus" in company with Morales, whose name appears alone in the title, and, more significantly, with Jacquet of Mantua who was a figure of considerable reputation in northern Italian circles as the principal musician in the ducal establishment at Mantua. Ruffo's knowledge of Jacquet's music is obvious from the fact that two of Ruffo's imitation Masses (one of them is the *Missa Aspice domine* included here) are based on motets by Jacquet.[10]

The *Missa Alma redemptoris mater* is a lengthy work for four equal voices with ample and extended contrapuntal procedures. The Mass as a whole is broadened in scope by means of elaborate sectional divisions of the Gloria, Credo, Sanctus, and Agnus Dei.

No polyphonic model has been found for this Mass, although it does show certain similarities to elements in Josquin's canonic four-voice setting of the *Alma redemptoris* antiphon published in Petrucci's *Motetti della Corona.*[11] While Ruffo's Mass does not seem to make sufficiently literal use of elements from Josquin's setting to warrant a claim of dependency, the *Missa Alma redemptoris* shows some signs of organization typical of many derived Masses of the time, especially those based on models having two sections. One of the clearest of these signs is the division of the Mass into two cycles of movements based on parallel material: the first cycle, based on the opening of the motet, is made up of the beginnings of the major divisions (Kyrie I, Et in terra, Patrem, Sanctus, Agnus I), and the second consists of the interior sections (Christe, Qui tollis, Et resurrexit, Et iterum, and Benedictus). The parallel material on which the second cycle of the *Missa Alma redemptoris* is based is the passage "Tu quae genuisti," in the antiphon (see *Antiphonale Romanum,* p. 65). Attempts to create symmetries and effective use of repetition, apart from those suggested by the Mass text itself, appear in the Domine deus, Benedictus, and Agnus I. Ruffo's basic approach throughout is one that stresses linear counterpoint, with only a few brief touches of chordal writing, all in the Gloria and Credo (e.g., Gloria, mm. 53 ff.; Qui tollis, mm. 20 ff., 49 ff.; Credo, mm. 99 ff.). For Ruffo this work offers an unusual emphasis on extended melodic fluidity, as at the end of the Crucifixus (mm. 20-24).

Missa Quem dicunt homines

This Mass and the one that follows (the *Missa Aspice domine*) appeared in Ruffo's collection of 1557 entitled *Messe di Vincentio Ruffo a Cinque Voci,* published by Antonio Gardano in Venice.[12] The present edition has the second (1565) edition of this Mass as its source (see Critical Notes). Mass prints were then rarities in the marketplace, and, if the absence of a dedication suggests publication without financial backing, this in turn encourages the surmise that Gardano had confidence in Ruffo's reputation. Such confidence may have been inspired by the publication of Ruffo's crowning madrigal print, the *Opera Nova di Musica,* in 1556.

The 1557 volume seems to reflect Ruffo's work as Mass composer after his return to Verona in the late 1540s and during his tenure as chapelmaster at the Cathedral. That Ruffo may have begun in the cathedral post as early as 1548 is suggested by the possibility that he intended this *Missa Quem dicunt hom-*

ines as a tribute to the Veronese Bishop Pietro Lippomano who served from 1544 to 1548. The model is a famous motet by Jean Richafort for the festival of Peter and Paul whose text makes special reference to Christ and Peter, thus suggesting a tribute to the institution of the Papacy. In Ruffo's case the Mass may well be a tribute to Bishop Lippomano. That the Mass has such a purpose is strongly suggested by the unusual treatment of its final Agnus Dei, in which Ruffo quotes the entire Superius of the second part of the Richafort motet, with its original text in which the name "Petrus" is prominent. Moreover, in view of the apparent intermingling of some of Ruffo's motets with those of Gombert during Ruffo's first Milanese period, it is striking to discover that the closest parallels to this procedure of quoting material from the model in a Mass are found in three Masses by Gombert: his Masses *Sancta Maria* and *Sur tous regrets* both use an entire voice-part from their respective models, while his Mass *Quam pulchra es* in its Agnus II uses the cantus firmus *Ecce sacerdos magnus* with its original text.

Richafort's motet had drawn the attention of many later composers, who used it as a basis for imitation Masses.[13] Mouton, Divitis, and an anonymous composer whose work is attributed to Josquin are perhaps the first, along with the composer of the work attributed to both Lupus and de Raedt; they are followed by Charles d'Argentilly, Morales, Ruffo, and Palestrina. Ruffo's setting of material from Richafort's motet exhibits reasonably close analogies to the setting by Morales (the only other five-voice setting) which had come out in 1544. In the distribution of certain motives, Ruffo may have been following Morales's lead.[14] Though Ruffo does not exhibit the imaginative use of rhythmic material from the model that Morales does, and though Ruffo's work lacks Palestrina's consistency of linear and contrapuntal writing, the *Missa Quem dicunt homines* shows Ruffo's solid grasp of derivation procedures and of five-voice contrapuntal reworking of the four-voice model.

Missa Aspice domine

This is one of two imitation Masses (the other is the *Missa Salvum me fac*) in the 1557 collection based on five-voice motets by Jacquet of Mantua, with whom, as we have suggested, Ruffo may have had a personal connection. It is indeed striking that these same motets were also used by Palestrina for five-voice Masses, and that both of these Masses also came out in a single collection—Palestrina's second book of Masses of 1567. The motet *Aspice domine* had been first issued by Jacques Moderne in 1532, and it was one of the most widely dissemi-

nated of the motets of Jacquet, being frequently reprinted and copied into manuscripts in Spain, Italy, Germany, and even England. In addition to Palestrina and Ruffo, a third composer, de Monte, also treated this motet as a Mass model. A comparison of settings by these composers points up Ruffo's tendency to make lavish use of the model's thematic content along with considerable freedom in distributing the motivic content of the motet within the Mass. As in the other imitation Masses in this edition, Ruffo's choice of motive for a particular segment of the Mass, when not affected by cyclic considerations, is governed at times by verbal or grammatical parallels between motet text and Mass text. Thus, the motive in the model for the word "Domine" appears in the Mass for passages on "Domine deus" in both the Gloria and Sanctus; the "sedet in tristitia" motive of the model comes up at "Qui sedes" in the Mass; and the motive for "quia facta est" is used for the Mass passages "per quem omnia facta sunt," "et homo factus est," "passus et sepultus est," and "qui locutus est."

Four Later Masses

The four works in Part II of this edition are transcribed from three late publications of Ruffo's Masses. The first two of these Masses were printed in Ruffo's *Missae Quatuor Concinate ad Ritum Concilii Mediolani* of 1570; the third, called *Missa de De profundis*, is from his *Messe a Cinque Voci*, known only in its reprint of 1580 (see below); and the last, *Missa Sanctissimae Trinitatis*, is from his *Quarto Libro di Messe a Sei Voci*, securely dated 1574. His last Mass print, the *Missae Boromeae* of 1592, is evidently a posthumously assembled compilation of works which was published as a tribute to Ruffo's association with Archbishop Carlo Borromeo. Borromeo's fame was then rising at such a pace that within a mere eighteen years after this print appeared he was canonized. The *Missae Boromeae* reprints the *Missa de De profundis* along with two other, untitled Masses. All of these works may have been written during the early 1570s, before Ruffo's departure from Milan.

Missa Quarti toni and Missa Octavi toni

The choice of these two Masses from the experimental Mass collection of 1570 deliberately complements an earlier publication, and thus makes available in transcription the full contents of this important volume. In 1963 Giuseppe Vecchi published the first volume of an announced *Opera Omnia* of Vincenzo Ruffo, which contained the first two Masses of this 1570 collection.[15] Since then, however, no further volumes of the projected edition have appeared, and it seems unlikely that it is to be continued in the near future.

The Council of Milan mentioned in the title of the print (see Plate I) was convoked by Borromeo in the autumn of 1565, soon after his own arrival in Milan. This Council reaffirmed the directives of the recently ended Council of Trent and sought to apply these principles locally in various fields, including sacred music. The Council of Milan decreed the avoidance of secular melodies in sacred music, and insisted that "pious and distinct music" was to be used in church "so that at once the words shall be understood and the listeners aroused to piety." The Council also ruled that singers should, if possible, be clerics, and that only the organ was to be used.[16]

All four Masses contained in Part II of this edition fulfill the first of these prescriptions to the letter. From the preface to Ruffo's 1570 volume, quoted earlier, we know that he had written one of these Masses (we do not know which one) in the spring of 1565 in response to Borromeo's demand, sent from Rome through the Milanese vicar Nicolo Ormaneto. Ruffo explains that he later imitated that first sample and when he had collected four such works, enough to fill a volume, he published them with Borromeo's permission. He evidently also had help from the Milanese Senator, Antonello Arcimboldo, to whom the dedication is addressed.

The 1570 Masses are short, four-voice compositions of extreme simplicity. Their titles indicate that they use neither polyphonic models nor any of the other well-known methods of Mass derivation, such as plainsong melodies or plainsong cycles, but are based on the familiar linear patterns and intervallic spans of the respective modes. For the layout of these Masses Ruffo adheres to two basic models, each of which is exemplified in the two Masses included here. In the Masses *Primi toni* and *Quarti toni* he sets most movements for four voices, but includes two three-voice interludes (the Crucifixus and Benedictus), and closes with added sonority by writing the second Agnus Dei statement for five voices. The second formal scheme (in the Masses *Secundi toni* and *Octavi toni*) is more severe. It entails a four-voice setting for all movements except the Benedictus, which is for three voices. In the Gloria and Credo settings of all these Masses, Ruffo sticks tightly to an austere chordal setting that is broken only occasionally by brief touches of contrapuntal relief. The obvious aim in the Gloria and in the Credo is to afford the listener full perception of the text, for which carefully framed declamatory patterns are found that differ somewhat from Mass to Mass. In an effort to avoid or mitigate the monotony resulting from such a style, Ruffo uses every device

that could vary the texture. Frequently used techniques are alternating smaller vocal groups with one another and with the entire ensemble, often using the *tutti* for a cumulative effect, and pacing the alternation procedure so as to set off certain phrases of text. The movements surrounding the Gloria and Credo, in which textual clarity is a lesser problem, remain more varied regarding contrapuntal and chordal technique. Yet here too, in all but the *Missa Quarti toni*, Ruffo uses long stretches of chordal writing even in the Kyries.

In the *Missa Quarti toni* Ruffo experiments with several structural features: The first Kyrie statement opens with simultaneous imitation of two motives by paired voices, establishing the characteristic intervals of the Fourth Mode, and the same style is applied to the second Kyrie statement. In the Christe, an ostinato figure in the Bass, consisting of the descending scalar octave of the Fourth Mode once transposed, is stated five times, with diminution and double diminution in its last two appearances. Above the ostinato, the upper voices provide a series of changing "realizations." This movement fits in with the wider use of Kyries as occasions for structural experimentation in late-sixteenth-century Masses. All four of these later Masses represent a drastic departure from Ruffo's earlier procedures, as they are governed by a sense of conformity to externally imposed criteria. In carrying out the ideals of the Council of Trent, Ruffo succeeds in achieving both clarity and euphony, as his preface puts it; but in reducing the musical resources in these Masses so drastically, especially in the Gloria and Credo, the inevitable limitations of so strict an approach become apparent. However, it is precisely this limitation of resources that gives these works substantial historical importance: in the broad expanse of late-sixteenth-century sacred music these Masses are among the works most fully shaped according to definable external purposes and aims.

Missa de De profundis

This Mass is transcribed here from its first known publication, a reprint of Ruffo's *Messe a Cinque Voci*, "composti secondo la forma del Concilio Tridentino." This collection is known only in its edition of 1580 (Brescia: Vincenzo Sabbio), but that edition is expressly said to be "diligently purged in this edition of many errors that were in the first."[17] No copy of the earlier version is known, and we can only surmise that it would have been issued about 1572, between the first "reform" Masses of 1570 and Ruffo's *Quarto Libro* of 1574. A publication date of ca. 1572 would readily explain why the 1574 print is called the "fourth" book. That the *Messe a Cinque*

Voci are from Ruffo's Milanese period (which ended in late 1572) is also indicated in the preface to the collection, in which the Milanese publisher Antonio Antoniano praises these Masses as being products of the stimulus given to Ruffo by Borromeo, "when he impelled Vincenzo Ruffo to this task." Antoniano adds, "Their utility has spread not only into our diocese but into many others."[18] This volume, too, consists of four works: an untitled Mass; a *Missa de Feria;* a *Missa a Voce Pari;* and the *Missa de De profundis.* Movements from the first two Masses listed were published by Torchi (1897), and the entire *Missa a Voce Pari* was published by R. J. Snow in 1958. Thus, the present edition offers the only Mass of this set for which no modern edition, in part or whole, has yet been available.[19]

The title, *Missa de De profundis,* is not an error. It appears in this form at the beginning of the work, in each part-book, and at the top of each page. There is no reason to believe that the title refers to any polyphonic antecedent for this Mass, nor does it seem to be a paraphrase of any known setting of the text *De profundis* of Psalm 129. The explanation of this title may lie simply in the unusually low disposition of voices in this work: the four principal voices remain in low tessitura throughout, and the Quintus, normally in Ruffo's five-voice Masses a second Tenor, is here a second Bassus, in baritone clef. That this was an established symbolic way of reflecting the *De profundis* text is clear from one of Josquin's two motets on the text, which is written, as Glarean noted, in clefs that indicate very low registers.[20] And that this tessitura was indeed too low for some choirs is suggested strongly by the second publication of the Mass in Ruffo's *Missae Boromeae* (1592) where it appears a fifth higher and the title is dropped.

The explicit thematic connection of Kyrie I and Sanctus in the *Missa de De profundis* is reminiscent of Palestrina's practice in several Masses (especially his *Missa Brevis,* published in 1570) that have no known antecedents. The five-voice texture of the *Missa de De profundis* afforded Ruffo greater scope for contrapuntal expansion and for subdivision of vocal groups than did the 1570 Masses. However, the disparity in approach between the austerity of the long central movements and the more polyphonic Kyrie, Sanctus, and Agnus Dei sections seems greater in the *Missa de De profundis* than in the 1570 compositions.

Missa Sanctissimae Trinitatis

The last Mass of this edition comes from Ruffo's large and impressive late collection, the *Quarto Libro di Messe a Sei Voci,* the Masses of which, as Ruffo says in the preface to this collection, were "conceived in Milan and brought forth in Pistoia." We can therefore believe that these works were written or at least begun in Milan before he left in 1572; the publication has a dedication to the canons of the Pistoian cathedral and dates from early in 1574. Their companion volume is his set of *Salmi Suavissimi et Devotissimi,* dedicated a month later to the Archbishop of Florence. Both of these prints mention their adherence to the decrees of the Trent Council, and the Mass volume contains, besides its dedication, an extended "Discourse to the Reader" in which Ruffo reaffirms his intention to find a means of composition that would satisfy the demands of intelligibility and piety laid down by the Tridentine decrees and later directed to him by Borromeo.

The four six-voice Masses of the 1574 collection are these: *Missa Sancti Jacobi* (for the patron saint of Pistoia); the present Mass, for the festival of the Holy Trinity; an imitation Mass, *Missa Tulerunt dominum meum,* based on one of Ruffo's own motets; and a very long *Missa Mortuorum,* which includes an extended setting of the *Dies Irae.* The *Missa Sanctissimae Trinitatis* shows a freer approach to the structure of the cycle than had been normal for the earlier "intelligible" Masses, and the compositional style blends homophony with more animated contrapuntal passages, especially in the Gloria and Credo; a good example of this use of counterpoint occurs in the last section of the Credo, from "Confiteor" to the end (mm. 51 ff.). Ruffo is clearly now seeking a better balance between the requirements of simplicity and clarity, on the one hand, and of musical artifice on the other.

Editorial Procedures

This edition follows, in the main, the procedures adopted in other volumes in this series. Although modern clefs are used, the originals are consistently indicated in incipits. Original note-values are reduced by half, except in passages in triple mensuration, where notes following the signatures $\Phi 3$ or $\mathcal{C} 3$ are reduced fourfold. This deviation from frequent editorial practice is based not on doubt that the sesquialtera proportion ($\mathbf{o} = \mathbf{o}\cdot$) is a more appropriate interpretation than tripla ($\mathbf{\sigma} = \mathbf{o}\cdot$), but on the view that modern performers may be more likely to interpret the proportional relationships at suitable tempi when the standard metrical unit, in modern notation, is the same in both duple and triple meters. Editorial accidentals have been inserted according to principles by now widely known and much discussed. Although space precludes justification of each such accidental, I refer the reader to discussions of the historical and methodological status of the so-called "rules" of musica ficta, in other publications.[21]

Critical Notes

Abbreviations used in the Critical Notes are as follows: M = Measure; B = Breve; SB = Semibreve; SM = Semiminim; L = Longa.

Missa Alma redemptoris mater

Gloria—M. 41, Cantus, clef changes to C2 after beat 2. Mm. 59-62, Altus, the text is indicated only by a repetition sign, but cannot mean that the previous clause should be repeated. Mm. 66, Bassus, beat 4 is f. M. 67, Bassus, beat 1 is g. M. 11, Tenor, note 1 is SM. Credo—M. 24, Bassus, note 2 is g. M. 26, Cantus, clef changes to C2 after beat 2. M. 38, Altus, sharp sign (meaning natural) inserted in print on first line of staff, interpreted here as a warning sign. M. 51, Altus, note 1 is f. M. 224, all voices, mensuration sign is "3." Sanctus—M. 29, Altus, notes 3 and 4 are SB's. Agnus Dei—M. 101, the phrase *"Laus Deo Finis"* is printed at the end of the Superius part in the 1542 volume.

Missa Quem dicunt homines

Since only the Cantus and Tenor parts of the 1557 edition are extant, this edition is derived from the second edition, of 1565. Gloria—M. 136, all voices, mensuration sign is Ⓞ3. Sanctus—M. 75, all voices, mensuration sign is Ⓞ3. Credo—M. 28, Tenor, beat 1 is e. Agnus Dei—M. 15, Tenor, beats 1-2, SB-rest misprinted as B-rest. M. 24, Altus, note 3 is SB. M. 38, all parts, in this Agnus Dei II, the Sexta pars is identical to the Superius of the Secunda pars of the Richafort motet, and the motet text is printed in the Mass publication as it appears here.

Missa Aspice domine

Kyrie—M. 11, Tenor, beats 1 and 2, SB-rest omitted in print. Credo—M. 3, Superius, notes 1 and 2 are SB's.

Missa Quarti toni

Kyrie—M. 16, Bassus, note 2 is misprinted as SB. Gloria—Mm. 25-26, all voices, the text repetition on the word *"tuam"* is specified in the print. Mm. 49-50, Tenor, in this voice only the last two notes are a dotted B and L, creating the suspension in m. 50. M. 98, Altus and Tenor have signature ₵3; Superius and Bassus have signature Ⓞ3. Credo—M. 37, Superius, meaningless signature ₵ inserted after B, g. M. 133, Tenor, note 2 printed as B. M. 191, Superius, note 1 wrongly omitted in print. Sanctus—M. 30, Tenor, note 3 misprinted as e. Agnus Dei—M. 9, Cantus, notes 1 and 2 misprinted as e, f. Mm. 14-18, Cantus, print indicates repetition of previous text, which would not fit other voices. Mm. 28-54, Tenor II printed in Superius part. M. 51, Superius, B, g, printed as SB.

Missa Octavi toni

Kyrie—M. 5, Tenor, g misprinted as f. Credo—M. 90, Superius, mensuration sign lacking; Altus, first clef in part misprinted as Tenor clef, thereafter normal. M. 119, Altus and Bassus have signature ₵3, while other parts have Ⓞ3. M. 121, Altus, note 1 omitted in print. Sanctus—Mm. 26-27, Superius, dot after c, B, interpolated. M. 38, Altus, final note omitted in print. M. 43, Altus, note 2 missing in print. Agnus Dei—M. 22, Bassus, final g omitted in print, previous C, breve, given as last note with fermata.

Missa de De profundis

Credo—M. 175, dot omitted in print after note 1, d. M. 205, Quintus, SB-rest wrongly inserted after note 2 in print. M. 209, Tenor, note 3 misprinted as SB.

Missa Sanctissimae Trinitatis

Credo—M. 114, Sextus, g misprinted as a.

Acknowledgments

For the provision of microfilms needed to transcribe these works I am indebted to Jena, Universitäts-Bibliothek; Bologna, Civico Museo Bibliografico Musicale; Professor Edward E. Lowinsky (who provided me with his own film of the *Missae Quatuor* of 1570, from the unique copy in the Biblioteca Capitolare, Pistoia); London, British Museum; Venice, Biblioteca Marciana. I am indebted to Mr. George Bozarth, and also to Mr. Thomas Hall, whose computer system for music printing is here employed for the first time. I am also grateful to the editors of A-R Editions for their unsurpassed patience and courtesy.

Lewis Lockwood
Princeton University

February 1979

Notes

1. See Lewis Lockwood, *The Counter-Reformation and the Masses of Vincenzo Ruffo*, Studi di Musica Veneta, vol. 2 (Venice: Fondazione Giorgio Cini, Istituto di Lettere Musica e Teatro, 1970).

2. Giuseppe Turrini, *La Tradizione Musicale a Verona* (Verona, 1954), p. 34.

3. The documentation for Ruffo's career available up to 1970 was used in Lockwood, *The Counter-Reformation*, Chapter 1. The new material discovered by Paganuzzi is reported in his article "Documenti Veronesi su Musicisti del XVI e XVII Secolo" in *Scritti in onore di Monsignore Giuseppe Turrini* (Verona, 1973), pp. 570-573.

4. On Ruffo's service with Alfonso d'Avalos, see Lockwood, *The Counter-Reformation*, pp. 19-26.

5. See Nicolai Gombert, *Opera Omnia*, ed. Joseph Schmidt-Görg (American Institute of Musicology, 1968), VII: ix.

6. On Ruffo as madrigalist see especially W. Wtorczyk, "Die Madrigale Vincenzo Ruffos" (Ph.D. diss., Freie Universität Berlin, 1955).

7. For a recent discussion of this long-contested matter, see Lockwood, ed., *Palestrina, Pope Marcellus Mass* (Norton Critical Scores: New York, 1975), pp. 34-36, and the 16th- and 17th-century documents published in translation in this work.

8. For the original text of this entire preface see Lockwood, *The Counter-Reformation*, pp. 237 ff., and for a facsimile see *MGG*, Vol. 11: col. 1078.

9. Lockwood, ed., *Palestrina, Pope Marcellus Mass*, pp. 82-85, and further discussions cited there.

10. On Jacquet as motet composer, see George E. Nugent, "The Jacquet Motets and Their Authors" (Ph.D. diss., Princeton University, 1973).

11. Petrucci, *Motetti della Corona* (Werken van Josquin des Prez, 1519), III: *Motetten*, No. 38.

12. This collection was first issued by Gardano in 1557, then reprinted by him in 1565 and again by Claudio Merulo da Correggio in 1567; for surviving copies see Lockwood, *The Counter-Reformation*, p. 237. For a critical edition of the Richafort motet see *Das Chorwerk*, Heft 94.

13. On these Masses see Lockwood, *The Counter-Reformation*, pp. 146-161.

14. I have provided a more detailed comparison of treatment of material in these two Masses and in the one by Palestrina in my monograph. See Lockwood, *The Counter-Reformation*, pp. 165-175.

15. *Vincentii Ruffi, Opera Omnia. I. Missae. [vol.] 3.a. Missae Quatuor Concinate ad Ritum Concilii Mediolani (1570)*, ed. Joseph Vecchi (Bologna, 1963). For full bibliographic particulars on this print and those that follow, see Lockwood, *The Counter-Reformation*, pp. 237-243.

16. For the texts of these decrees see *Acta Ecclesiae Mediolanensis* (Milan, 1891-1897), II: 99, 186, 255, 391, 403 ff.; also E. Cattaneo, "Note Storiche sul Canto Ambrosiano," *Archivio Ambrosiano* (1950), III: 68-75.

17. Lockwood, *The Counter-Reformation*, p. 239.

18. Ibid.

19. L. Torchi, ed., *L'Arte Musicale in Italia* (Milan, 1897), I: 193-204 (publishing the Et in terra of the *Missa Sine Nomine* and the Patrem of the *Missa de Feria*); the edition by R.J. Snow of the *Missa a Voce Pari* is in the series *Musica Liturgica*, I.1 (1958).

20. O. Strunk, *Source Readings in Music History* (New York, 1950), pp. 222 ff.

21. The full title of the print containing the *Missa Alma redemptoris* is: *Missae Cum Quatuor Vocibus Decantandae, Morales Hispani, Ac Aliorum Authorum in hac scientia non vulgarium . . . Venetiis apud Hieronimum Scotum. 1542.* For extant copies see the *Répertoire International des Sources Musicales, Recueils Imprimés, XVIᵉ-XVIIᵉ Siècles* (München-Duisburg, 1960), p. 136.

CANTVS.

·VINCENTII RVFFI·

MODERATORIS ECCLESIAE
MAIORIS MEDIOLANI.

MISSÆ QVATVOR CONCINATE
AD RITVM CONCILII MEDIOLANI.

QVATVOR  VOCVM.

MEDIOLANI.

Apud Antonium Antonianum. 1570.

Plate I. Title page of Ruffo's *Missae Quatuor Concinate ad Ritum Concilii Mediolani*, 1570.
(From copy in Biblioteca Capitolare, Pistoia)

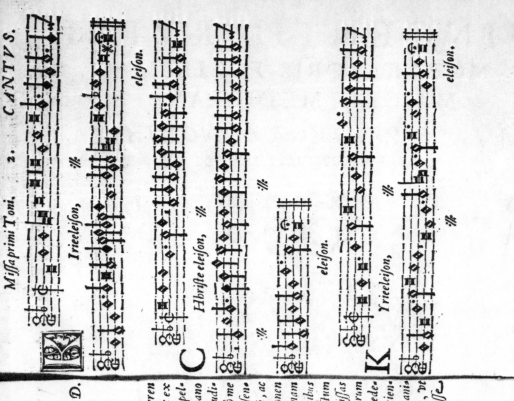

CANTVS.

Missa primi Toni. 2.

Irieeleison, eleison.

Christe eleison, eleison.

Kyrieeleison, eleison.

ILLVSTRI ET MVLTVM REVER. D.
Antonello Arcimboldo Senatori dignissimo Mediolani.

Vincentius Ruffus. S. P. D.

VM cogerer id oneris suscipere, quod Illust. & Reueren
diss. Cardinalis Borrhomaeus olim mihi imposuerat, vt ex
sancti tridentini Concilij decreto Missas (sic enim appel-
lantur) aliquot conficerem, quae ita omni profano, ac vano
modorum cultu carerent, & vocum ille tantus, & tam dulcis sonus audi-
torum aures piè, religiosè, sanctèq; implerent, & demulcerent; Quò me
verterem, penitus ignorabam: Tu tandem aliquando, qui eiusdem sen-
tentiae fueras, obuiam mihi prodijsti, sensumq; tuum aperiè praetulisti, ac
tanquam (vt ita dicam) Protoplastes huiusce modi symphoniam componen-
di modum mihi indicasti. Itaq; cohortatione tua ductus Missam vnam
ita confeci, vt syllabarum numeri, simulq; voces, & modi ab auditoribus
piis planè, & perspicuè noscerentur, ac perciperentur. Ex quo factum
fuit, vt exemplar illud imitando in posterum ad alias istiusmodi Missas
conficiendas facilior, promptiorq; essem: Quas cum in certam numerum
redigissem, atq; idem Illustriss. & Reuerendiss. Borrhomaeus, vt ede-
rem, mihi mandasset, tibi dicare volui, vt quibus huiusmodi opus conficien-
di rationem, & viam mihi ostendisses. Has igitur accipe eo hilari ani-
mo, & laeto vultu, quo ego largè, liberaliterq; dono: Ita enim fiet, vt
summam meam obseruatiam, qua te semper colui, tibi nunquam defuisse
significem. Vale.

Plate II. Dedication and first page of Ruffo's *Missae Quatuor Concinate ad Ritum Concilii Mediolani*, 1570. (From copy in Biblioteca Capitolare, Pistoia)

SEVEN MASSES
Part I: Three Early Masses

Missa Alma redemptoris mater

4

[Sanctus]

Osanna ut supra

[Agnus Dei]

30

34

Laus Deo Finis

Missa Quem dicunt homines

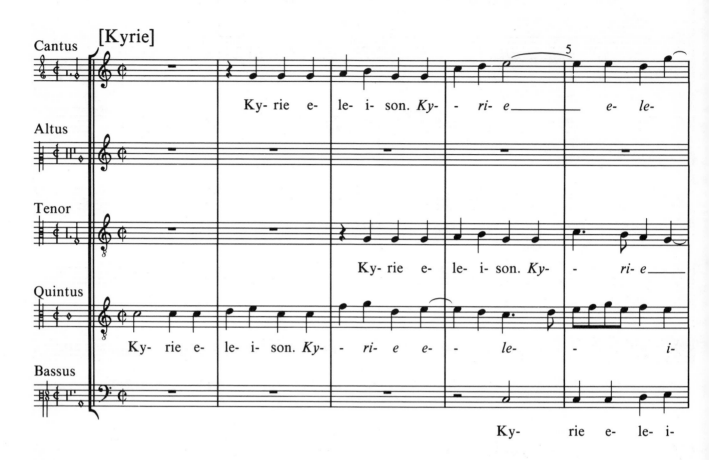

40

42

[Gloria]

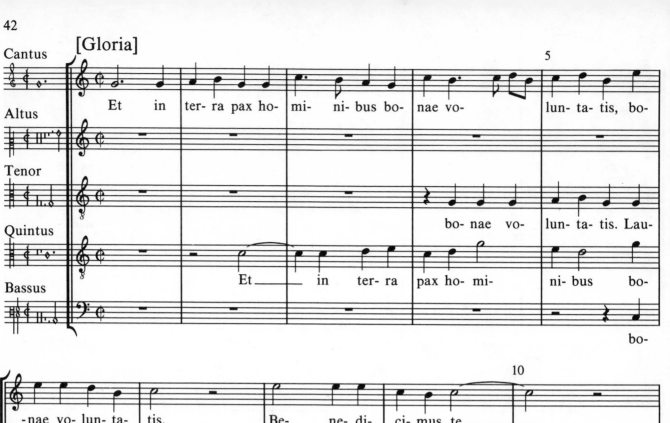

Cantus: Et in ter- ra pax ho- mi- ni- bus bo- nae vo- lun- ta- tis, bo-

Altus:

Tenor: bo- nae vo- lun- ta- tis. Lau-

Quintus: Et in ter- ra pax ho- mi- ni- bus bo-

Bassus: bo-

-nae vo- lun- ta- tis. Be- ne- di- ci- mus te.

bo- nae vo- lun- ta- tis. Lau- da- mus te. Be- ne- di-

-da- mus te. Be- ne- di- ci- mus te. A- do- ra-

-nae vo- lun- ta- tis. Lau- da- mus te. Be- ne- di- ci- mus te.

-nae vo- lun- ta- tis. Lau- da- mus te. Be- ne- di- ci-

A- do- ra- mus te. Glo-

-ci- mus te. A- do- ra- mus te. Glo- ri-

- mus te. Glo- ri- fi- ca- mus te.

A- do- ra- mus te. Glo- ri- fi- ca-

-mus te. A- do- ra- mus te. Glo- ri- fi- ca-

46

52

54

62

[Agnus Dei]

Osanna ut supra

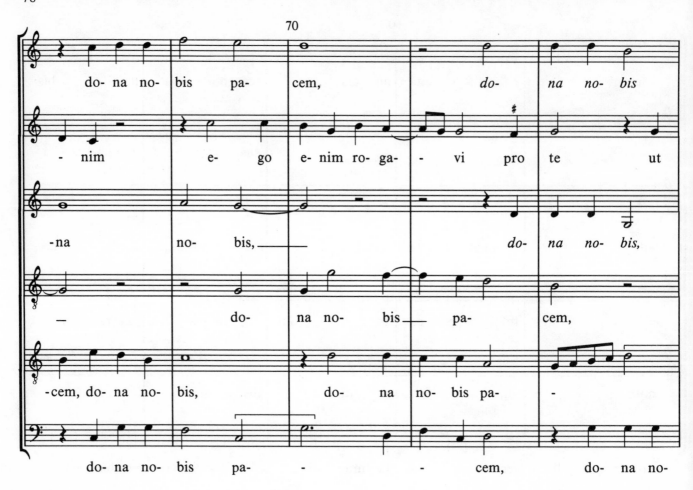

Missa Aspice domine

[Gloria]

Cantus
Altus
Tenor
Quintus
Bassus